BEING EVE IN ADAM'S WORLD

The Journey of Struggle to Triumph

CASEY ALEXIS

CASEY ALEXIS

BEING EVE IN ADAM'S WORLD

This is a work of creative nonfiction. Some parts have been fictionalized in varying degrees, for various purposes. Any resemblance to actual persons, living or dead, events, or locales is entirely coincidental.

Copyright © 2020 by Casey Alexis

All rights reserved. No part of this book may be reproduced or used in any manner without the written permission of the copyright owner except for the use of quotations in a book review. For more information, address: Casey@beingeve.info.

First paperback edition August 2020

ISBN: 978-1-7356211-0-4 (paperback)
ISBN 978-1-7356211-1-1 (eBook)

www.beingeve.com

CASEY ALEXIS

This book was written and dedicated to every woman, wife, mother, sister, and friend.

God loves you, and so do I.

To my dear husband and children, my greatest gift and highest calling, thank you.

CASEY ALEXIS

Contents

Introduction   9
1. The Missing Piece in Perfection   15
2. When Life Brings Death   30
3. A Father's Love   41
4. The Reality of it All   52
5. The Blame Game & The Scapegoat   67
6. The End of a Fairytale   80
7. The Present Changes the Future   91
8. Life Goes On   104
9. The Redemption in Motion   113
10. As it was In the Beginning   123

NOTES   132
INDEX   137

CASEY ALEXIS

INTRODUCTION

Imagine for a second what it must've been like to be born into a world made exclusively for a man...

I am sure most of you are probably saying to yourself, *"I don't have to imagine it. I see this every day."* In every facet of life, most people would probably agree that it would be challenging to find something that is not entirely male-dominated. Whether it is a sport or a specific industry, our male counterparts have always held a more dominant position in American society. Times have changed and are continuously evolving as we see more and more women in areas and fields that were once entirely male-driven. While some of us may say we haven't come far enough, we can all agree that women have come a long way from the days of "being seen and not heard." Whichever way you decide to examine women's history, the present-day woman no longer resembles the woman of the past. Women are no longer asking for permission to have a seat at the table--they're demanding one. If necessary, they will build their table from scratch. And if you try to stop it, be ready, because more than likely, there is a tribe of women ready and willing to join forces to create a space without question.

The collective strength, when women gather to impact change or to support a cause, is a force to be reckoned with. From Harriet Tubman and the underground railroad to the beginning of the

Women's Rights Movement, up until this very day, the ability to gather as a collective group to demand change is truly one of our superpowers. On the opposite side of the spectrum, we tend to be the most vulnerable when we are alone. Most women, or if I could be so bold and say all women, can probably attest to a time in their lives where they experienced moments of vulnerability. It was in those moments we felt the most alone, battling adverse thoughts and emotions. It was in those moments where some of us experienced our innocence tragically taken away. It was in those moments where our womanhood was challenged by those who had the advantage of power. It was in those moments where our enemies patiently waited for an opportunity to strike. Those moments of vulnerability may still have a hold on us, and we often think of what we could have done differently. Asking ourselves, *"where did I go wrong?"* Regardless of how many times we cross-examined ourself, it never changes the fact that those moments occurred, and that they changed the course of our story.

Here lies the reason why this book came to be. During the pinnacle point of the worst year in my marriage, I wrote down the title of this book. When I finally decided to transition this book from heart to paper, I must admit, the first draft came from a place of hardship. The more I wrote, the more hurt, pain, and disdain of life's experiences as a woman kept pouring out of me. The fantastic thing about the entire process was that the more I filled those pages, the more I began to heal. The more I recovered, the more my perspective changed. I realized that although those painful moments in my story did occur, they certainly didn't have to stain my entire story, and they most certainly didn't have the right to define me. I walked away with a change in my whole worldview. It was then that I learned how my past had shaped my entire perspective. I was looking at life from a skewed point of view; I looked at life through pain-colored glasses.

It's astonishing to think that how we view our world has a startling effect on how we do just about everything when it comes to living. Think about it for a minute: both the positive and negative moments in our lives have defined, shaped, and impacted the way we do life, relationships, our careers, and the way we live in society. Within my life, I came to understand it fully, so much so, I decided to deep dive into my story. Once I did that, I decided to take it a bit further and examine the stories of other women around me. I even went as far as taking my observations on social media. I came away with one great revelation: our stories are not that different. Life happens to us all, and it may happen to us at different times of our lives. It may look a little different because of ethnicity, cultural differences, and financial status, but for the most part, the stories are not that different. Even with this realization, as women, we tend to be the hardest on ourselves and each other. So, I decided to go back to the book that described in detail the starting point of womanhood. I went back to the Bible. I wanted to examine the story of the woman who started it all, Eve.

Why start with Eve? Well, from the biblical standpoint of creation, Eve was the first woman to walk the face of the earth. I wanted to examine the life of the first woman to see if my observations regarding our similarities were correct. And to be honest, I was inquisitive; I wanted to delve into her story without the focus being all on Adam. Typically, when I would read the creation story, my attitude towards her came with a very long 'eye roll' for the one that caused it all. The Fall began from her decision, which caused a rippling effect, forever changing her and the entire world to follow. When I would read the story of creation, I had a list of 'should-haves' and 'could-haves' that would have resulted in a better outcome than the one that Momma Eve dished out to the rest of us. I had a list of judgments against her, and at one point, I believed if the shoe were on the other foot, I would have known better, or I would have done better. Thankfully, life was kind enough to teach me a few things, while simultaneously smacking me in the head. As I began to read Eve's story with an open heart, as well as reflecting on my own, I understood how that one moment defined Eve's narrative. And because of it, I was missing out on a tremendous opportunity to learn from her. When I decided to drop the self-proclaimed righteousness, I was shocked to see how many similarities there were. I was able to see me in many of the life challenges she experienced. And quite frankly, I believe every single woman will see their reflection when they dive into her story.

Being Eve in Adam's World is the journey of one woman whose story has been told countless times throughout human history.

Unfortunately, Eve's narrative is minimized to the character who caused the most considerable upheaval within humanity. She usually is characterized as a victim who fell prey to the advances of a snake. As a result, her story preaches as a warning, yet never embraced as an experience. I encourage you to take this journey with me—a journey of discovery of finding you in the woman who started it all. Maybe take a close sister-friend with you, and let's embrace the journey together. As you read on, you will be able to see your reflection in the narrative of the first woman, the mother of all, who like some of us, experienced love, purpose, marriage, motherhood, fear, pain, death, betrayal, rejection and redemption.

CASEY ALEXIS

CHAPTER 1

THE MISSING PIECE IN PERFECTION

Although her story takes place in a different era, and it is also very short in the literary context of scripture, Eve's story has physically lived on through centuries of human experiences. There is not much we know about her, but there is so much we can learn from her. In this chapter, we are going to do a deep dive into the creation story. It's a must, considering how much of Eve's life is in the first couple of chapters of the Bible. Within this first chapter, you'll discover what God had in mind when He created Eve. As you uncover what He had in mind for her, you will also realize what He had in mind for YOU.

Eve, by biblical account, was named by her spouse Adam. She was to become the mother of all things living. According to biblical history, when Eve first made her appearance into the world, everything had already been spoken into existence and was utterly functional **(Genesis, Chapters 1-3).** Even the animals had previously been named. *"Imagine for a second what it must've been like to be born into a world made exclusively for a man..."* As we venture through Eve's journey, it is essential to capture why that statement is so important. It is in no way an attack on the creation story. It is an opportunity to learn what God had in mind when He first created Adam.

Genesis chapter 2 begins the story of Adam and Eve. The chapter opens with God breathing life into Adam, who was created from the dust of the earth. The story also gives us a glimpse into Adam's

relationship with God and his created purpose. As Adam cares for the planet and is naming all the animals, God realizes there is something a little off. Adam does not have a suitable mate. As a matter of fact, out of all the things God does within the time of creation, everything is good except for the fact that man is alone. As a result, He places Adam into a deep sleep, as the Bible explains in **Genesis 2:21-22:**
"So, the Lord God caused the man to fall into a deep sleep, and while he was sleeping, he took one of the man's ribs and closed up the place with flesh. Then the Lord God made a woman from the rib he had taken out of the man, and he brought her to the man."

The definition of the term alone, Merriam-Webster defines as "separated from others: isolated." God believed it wasn't good for Adam to be separate and isolated. Ladies, let's take a moment to enjoy the fact that God knew the world wouldn't be as good as without a woman's presence. He knew it wasn't beneficial for Adam to be alone, so he fashioned a partner that Adam would know was his own-- a woman created out of his own body. And, Adam knew it the moment he set his eyes on Eve. *"This is bone of my bones, flesh of my flesh; she shall be called woman for she was taken out of man."* Eve was everything God knew Adam would need, perfectly designed to help him thrive and have dominion while subduing and caring for the earth.

The symbolism used to describe what God removed from Adam to create Eve during the deep sleep was a rib. Naturally, I went and did some research on the physical attributes and function of the bones within the human body, and what I found was very interesting! For those of us that may be unfamiliar, the rib cage is a component of our respiratory system, with its primary function being to protect, support, and of course, to assist in respiration. The rib cage protects vital organs such as the heart, lungs, kidneys, liver, and major blood vessels found in the chest cavity of the body. These major organs are a necessity. Without these organs functioning properly, the human body cannot survive. I also began to investigate the function of the bone, as it is part of the skeletal frame of a human being. I added a snippet of the information here so you can understand why the rib was so significant.

Bone is often stereotyped as only a protective and supportive framework for the body. Though it does perform these functions, bone is a very dynamic organ that is constantly remodeling and changing shape to adapt to the daily forces placed upon it. Moreover, bone stores crucial nutrients, minerals, and lipids and produces blood cells that nourish the body and play a vital role in protecting the body against infection.

Bones have many functions, including the following:

Support: *Bones provide a framework for the attachment of muscles and other tissues.*

Protection: *Bones such as the skull and rib cage protect internal organs from injury.*

Movement: *Bones enable body movements by acting as levers and points of attachment for muscles.*

Mineral storage: *Bones serve as a reservoir for calcium and phosphorus, essential minerals for various cellular activities throughout the body.*

Blood cell production: *The production of blood cells, or hematopoiesis, occurs in the red marrow found within the cavities of individual bones.*

Energy storage: *Lipids, such as fats, stored in adipose cells of the yellow marrow, serve as an energy reservoir.*

What does all of that have to do with Eve? Well, God used the rib as a symbolic form of Eve's purpose. Unlike Adam, she wasn't formed from the earth. She was taken from what was already alive. As the woman to be the mother of all things living, I believe this symbolized that life would come from her. Being the symbolic rib in the Garden, she would be the source of life-- reproducing, protecting, supporting, and sustaining. When God fashioned Eve from Adam, it created a partnership like none other. The way they were formed and intricately designed allowed them to work in synergy, just as the human body requires all parts to work correctly for optimal function. Simply, Eve was purposed to sustain life, and Adam was intended to maintain life on earth. Let's take a quick look at the definition of both words:

Sustain (EVE) *- (verb) strengthen or support physically or mentally.* <u>Synonyms</u>*: comfort, help, assist, encourage, succor, support, give strength to, buoy up, carry, cheer up, hearten;*

Maintain (ADAM) *- (verb) cause or enable (a condition or state of affairs) to continue.* <u>Synonyms:</u> *preserve, conserve, keep, retain, keep going, keep alive, keep up, prolong, perpetuate, sustain, carry on, continue*

Eve's primary purpose was tied directly to Adam's. She was to him what Adam was to the earth. They were designed to operate so well together that as one would sustain or maintain, the other would also flourish. When you look at how God created them both, you will understand that Eve was not made to be lower than Adam, and Adam was not made to be smaller than Eve. They were both equals in what they were purposed to do. They both poured into each other to ensure that life on earth flourished! In allowing them to do just that, God leaves them both with clear instructions. In Genesis 2, God's directives state, **"*be fruitful and increase in number; fill the earth and subdue it.*"** He also instructed while in the Garden, **"*you are free to eat from any tree in the Garden, but you must not eat from the tree of the knowledge of good and evil, for when you eat from it, you will certainly die.*"**

Providing them with these two directives, He gave them both a plan, a purpose, and responsibility. These directives would probably feel more like rules for some, but if we examine it from the standpoint of a parent, God was guiding His children. What God said provided them the direction they needed to do what they were called to do, to maintain and sustain life on earth. How so? Well, to be fruitful and to increase in number will lead to growth. Anything that grows is proven to be alive and well. Now, let's address the second directive, the one that spoke directly to what they should and shouldn't consume. This directive gave them guidance on what was nourishing for the body. Again, guiding so they can flourish and build. There was also something a little extra added to the second directive that stood out. They were told not to eat from this one tree out of all the trees in the Garden, and if they did, they would surely die.

Although the directive was clear, the very presence of the tree of knowledge of good and evil revealed a fantastic truth. Even in the beginning, God allowed them to have the power of choice. **Genesis 2:9** says, *"The Lord God made all kinds of trees grow out of the ground—trees that were pleasing to the eye and good for food. In the middle of the Garden were the tree of life and the tree of the knowledge of good and evil."* True freedom comes with the power of choice, and with that freedom, Adam and Eve were presented with options. Having options gave them the authority to make decisions-- decisions that eventually will enable them to sustain, maintain, subdue, and have dominion on the earth. Without the power of choice, both Adam and Eve are reduced to a position likened to that of an innkeeper--someone who runs an environment but has zero input on how the environment should function and thrive, which did not align with God's original intent for their lives. To subdue and have dominion is to have control over, to overcome, and to establish sovereignty. Adam and Eve could not do that without the power of making decisions. Being created in the image of God and His likeness, I am sure He desired them to have authority over what they would subdue.

Being made perfect in God's image and their purpose, gave them authority in their perspective areas. Eve being the source of life, reproducing, protecting, supporting, and sustaining, she would more than likely manage the living in the Garden. As a matter of fact, because of her position, I would safely assume she interacted with all living things, which guides us into **Genesis, chapter 3**, where we find Eve in conversation with a Serpent. Now, if you are a bit taken aback by the bible's description of Eve chatting with a snake, just think about how many times you watched Cinderella talk to a couple of mice, or Aurora talking to birds. Get the drift, okay, let's move on.

Unbeknownst to Eve at the time, the Bible states the "Serpent was very crafty." It pulled Eve into a conversation and asked her a question she never heard before. *It said to the woman, "Did God really say, 'You must not eat from any tree in the Garden'?"* Being as crafty as it was, the Serpent did two things with that question. The first thing it did was impart doubt, implicating that there is a possibility that she heard incorrectly. The second and most dangerous thing it did was to imply that Eve lacked information, leaving her room to entertain the possibility that she was limited in knowledge. Eve, like many of us, would immediately respond with the directive given to her, and she adds the consequence of what would take place if she did eat from the tree.

With her response, the Serpent decides to kick it up a notch. It responded right back to her statement and said, *"you will not surely die... For God knows that when you eat from it, your eyes will be opened, and you will be like God, knowing good and evil."* (Genesis 3: 4-5). At that moment, the Serpent challenged her statement by implying God wasn't telling the whole truth, expounding on the previous idea that she was limited in knowledge in some way.

MY REFLECTION:

Have you ever had conversations like the one Eve had with 'the serpent'? Was it an internal battle, or was it with a "serpent" in your life? How many times have you heard, "did God say," in those situations? How often were those questions directed to your purpose, gifting, or calling? How has doubt affected your ability to live the life God has called for you to live?

_____
_____
_____
_____
_____
_____
_____
_____
_____
_____
_____
_____
_____
_____
_____
_____

I hope you took a moment on the <u>MY REFLECTION</u> questions. The idea behind the <u>MY REFLECTION</u> sections within the book allows you to step into Eve's journey and see your reflection. It is an opportunity to see what it was like for her because you know all too well what it's been like for you during your own life experiences. I encourage you to review each of these sections and allow it to be a mirror you use to examine yourself at your core. Write your answers down and take an opportunity to reflect.

Immediately after she heard those words of the Serpent, the Bible says Eve began to look at the tree differently, *"believing it was good for food, it was pleasing to the eye and desirable for gaining wisdom."* Once the Serpent skillfully introduces doubt, the possibility that she lacked knowledge, implied she was confined in some way. Eve began to see the tree as something she desired rather than believing what God told her, the tree would lead to death. I can only imagine her thoughts in that vulnerable moment when the tree became desirable, *"maybe God didn't tell me everything I needed to know. I mean, I was created after Adam. Everything was already created by the time I got here, and Adam got to name everything. I didn't get to name anything. Maybe this is my opportunity to be like God and know everything He knows."* By merely introducing the thought of a limitation, Eve's perspective changed. The Bible goes on to say, *"she took some and ate it."*

I'm pretty sure before the Serpent's arrival; Eve thought she knew everything she needed to know about life in the Garden. But the Serpent being crafty, appeared to present something new. The doubt the Serpent imparted was so captivating, Eve never went back to God to confirm whether the Serpent's words were valid. She was unaware of the power of doubt. Eve gained doubt and lost trust in the truth of God's directives. She put her faith in the new information she gained because it became appealing to the outcome she desired: the result of being just like God. *"For God knows that when you eat from it, your eyes will be opened, and you will be like God, knowing good and evil."*

Eve bought into the idea that she would become like God, neglecting the fact that she was created in His image and likeness. Being the mother of all things living with the full capability to develop and sustain life, Eve was very much like God. Unfortunately, when doubt came in, the truth became unclear, and she began to seek perfection from the perspective of the creation rather than the Creator. Not realizing her desire for perfection was futile, she ate the fruit and took on the exact opposite of what she was imperfection.

The Serpent seemed to be fully aware of the words required to feed into Eve, so she was found wanting what the Tree of Knowledge of Good and Evil had to offer. She fell right into the Serpent's trap, allowing it to succeed in making the woman doubt who she was. The entry of doubt was what the Serpent needed to unravel what God had in mind when He breathed life into Adam and fashioned Eve from his rib. The simple question, "did God say," was just the beginning of the deceitful plan to flip the entire world upside down.

> ## *Being Eve Lesson 1:*
>
> *I embodied the characteristics of life and life changed the moment I doubted and believed that I lacked something or was confined in some way.*
>
> Know who you are and the purpose you bring into every environment you were made to be a part of. Doubt diminishes your value and creates an opportunity for others to label you with what they perceive to be your worth. You must never allow creation to dictate who you are, rather seek your purpose from the Creator. Go back to the source of your strength, your creator, who knows who you are and the plans that he has for you. **(Jeremiah 29:11)**

BEING EVE IN ADAM'S WORLD

CHAPTER 2

WHEN LIFE BRINGS DEATH

Like Eve, we naturally bring life into the world, whether it is through the physical manifestation of child-bearing, or it is with our gifts, talents, and abilities. Women can naturally take anything that is withering and bring it back to life. Under normal circumstances, that's what we do. And when we aren't, it is safe to say, something life-altering more than likely occurred. With Eve it all started with words dipped in manipulation which birthed doubt. In some of us, it began with lies, abuse, and offenses that began to strip away at us. Those life-altering events can bring all forms of debilitating changes to the life of a woman. The changes can be life-long, some of them are unbearable, some of them pass the woman herself and transfers to those around her. Looking through the lens of Eve's journey, we will be able to see how the change that transpired in her began to affect those connected to her.

Genesis 3:6 "When the woman saw that the fruit of the tree was good for food and pleasing to the eye, and desirable for gaining wisdom, she took some and ate it."

Eve experienced a change of heart once she believed the idea that God perhaps didn't tell her the whole truth. That change of heart, was once known to lead to death, became pleasing to her eyes, and good enough to eat. She then followed that belief with action, she ate the fruit, and eventually gave it to Adam. The transaction of the fruit from Eve into Adam's hand always puzzled me. I never could fully grasp how it is that Adam heard the directive from God and so quickly disregard His words. Scripture says in **Genesis 3:6**, *"she also gave some to her husband, who was with her, and he ate it."*

There was no conversation between Adam and Eve, nor with Adam and the Serpent. This one line always had me scratching my head, like what? How could it have been that easy? I have heard many interpretations and explanations regarding the whereabouts of Adam during Eve's deception. Why did he allow this to happen? Did he challenge it, and the writer did not make mention of it? Did he idolize Eve and reject God's directives? All these questions with several different explanations and interpretations. And it was not until I began writing this book that I realized none of that mattered. The Bible mentioned what was necessary for the reader to take hold of. It wasn't said because it wasn't the focal point. The focal point within the story of their demise wasn't Adam's whereabouts; it was the transfer of the fruit from Eve to Adam.

The transfer was so simple and so easy, it almost seemed like it happened everyday…because it did! Adam simply ate because his wife gave him something to eat. Eve, more than likely, did this day in and day out, so why would he question the food she gave him that day? If you refer to what we discussed in the previous chapter, Eve was everything Adam needed, and Adam was everything she needed. They were in perfect accord in their purpose within the Garden of Eden, she sustained, and Adam maintained. So, why would Adam ever question Eve when she offered him something to eat? Her providing Adam sustenance was more than likely common practice within the Garden daily. The only thing that differed about this day was the fruit she gave him. The Bible doesn't make mention that once Eve ate the fruit, her appearance had changed. As a result, this leaves us to believe that the changes she experienced were all internal before it became external. Eve's mind changed, her heart followed to then proceeded with action, she ate, and then she transferred it in a way her husband never saw it coming.

MY REFLECTION:

Have you ever experienced a change of heart? Did your change of heart lead you to a change in behavior? What was the catalyst behind that change? How did it change you?

_____
_____
_____
_____
_____
_____
_____
_____
_____
_____
_____
_____
_____
_____
_____
_____
_____
_____
_____
_____
_____

I am sure many of us can relate to what happened in Eve when her thoughts began to shift from one idea to another. As our minds change, it may take a moment or two to change our hearts, but eventually, we will see the change begin to manifest in our behavior. An excellent example of this is when a woman finally decides to leave a relationship. The decision happens in her mind and impacts her heart way before the man ever sees a physical change in the relationship. When he finally does realize it's over, he more than likely is caught by surprise, not realizing that her heart had changed towards him a long time ago. By the time he finally realizes, it is probably too late. Just like a volcanic eruption, the changes in a woman's heart and mind takes place below the surface before it emerges at the top of the volcano's opening, not leaving much time for anyone to get out of its path.

The bible states that the mastermind behind Eve's demise was responsible for the transfer between her and Adam to unravel the Garden was crafty. The meaning of the word crafty is defined as "clever at achieving one's aims by indirect or deceitful methods." For the Serpent to achieve its aim, it needed to study the subjects very carefully. The Serpent was aware of the order in the Garden. It understood the nature of both the man and the woman; it knew their respective characteristics and how they were intricately designed to operate with one another. How do we know? We can see it in its plan of attack. The Serpent went for Eve because she was the most effective way to bring disorder into the Garden. Eve's life connected to Adam, and Adam's being connected to the earth, and both connected to God. Eve was the mother of all things living, and therefore she was the source that was the gateway for life within the Garden. Eve wasn't a more manageable approach because she was weak; she was the best approach because the Serpent knew how it all worked.

The Serpent understood the operational system within the Garden and used it to its advantage. Picture this for a moment: If you want to stop a machine from operating, the first thing you do is to look for its power source (the source that brings it to life). Once you figure out the power source, the next step would be to unplug it. The Serpent was fully aware that Eve was the source of life within The Garden, so its primary focus was to unplug her first. It knew if it were successful, there would be no need for an in-depth conversation with Adam; there would be no need to attempt any further deceitful methods. The Serpent used perfection within the Garden to gain the trust of Eve to entertain its conversation. She fell victim to what its words appeared to be at first glance, not realizing there was a whole heap of tragic mess to follow.

We can all probably think to a time when we fell victim to our own 'serpents' who watched from the sidelines and knew what we failed to know about ourselves. They slithered into our lives, hoping and waiting for the opportune time when we were the most vulnerable to inflict a bite filled with venom of lies, deceit, and manipulation. But like Eve, if we allow the words of anyone but God to impact who we are and the value we bring to any environment we step into, we won't ever fully know the gift that is within us. Just like Eve was a gateway to life in The Garden, we too carry that same ability in the environments that we are a part of. Every single one of us has the fantastic gift to be a part of an environment, career, sport, industry, etc., and bring life into that space in whatever capacity!

And just like Eve, the serpents we encounter have spoken words that make us feel inadequate and small. The more we think we are not good enough, the more they push their control. They sit, wait, and hope that we take the bate, believing that we need whatever it is they are offering.

Hoping that the feeling of inadequacy gives way to them be able to take from us at will. Hoping that we would eat whatever fruit they were dishing out. Hoping that it will give way for them to abuse or mistreat us.

Being a gateway to life is a gift. And because it is such a great gift, many seek to take it from us to empower themselves selfishly. They speak words that don't produce sustainable fruit, showing love masked in lust, display betrayal disguised in all forms of hatred, rape, harassment, abuse, and the list goes on and on.

The reason it occurs is to diminish what God placed in us from the very beginning of our existence. And it doesn't just end with us. The main goal is to have us become the opposite of what we are created to be--to become a gateway to death rather than life. To do that, it would require us to believe that we are inadequate, that we are less than, that we are not who the Creator deemed us to be. The goal is to have us believe it in our thoughts so it can change our hearts, and eventually, we will begin to act outside of our true nature. As a result, the gift no longer is seen as a gift but a curse. We become carriers of things that destroy rather than build. We quickly speak death rather than life. It's easier to hold on to emotions like hatred, jealousy, and resentment instead of love, trust, and forgiveness. Eventually, the feelings and emotions of inadequacy, hatred, jealousy, and all those other things will begin to spread because misery loves company. It spreads to those we love; it spreads to our children; it spreads in our home, and then into in every area of our lives. Hence the famous quote, "hell has no fury like a woman scorned." That's the end goal-to scorn us, and like Eve, be quickly passed on from one hand into another hand and another.

> **_Being Eve Lesson 2:_**
>
> *I experienced a change that not only changed me, but eventually carried death to the man I loved, and eventually to those we loved, as well as the earth we were caring for.*
>
> The amount of greatness in one woman can embody an entire generation, and her innate capabilities can change her entire sphere of influence. This power can also become our greatest weapon when used with a heart that desires death rather than life. The greatest way to prevent the latter, is to ask ourselves whether we are living out our life's purpose. Are we living life exuding life in our behavior or death? As we begin to analyze our actions, we must remember that the choices offered come with their own share of consequences, so choose wisely. Let us always choose life. **(Deuteronomy 28)**

CASEY ALEXIS

CHAPTER 3

A FATHER'S LOVE

Before we dive deep into the consequences of Adam and Eve's demise, I wanted to take a moment to address the love of a father. The creation story reminds me of a father's desire to provide the very best for his children. I enjoy the book of Genesis because it gives you a glimpse of what the Creator God had in mind when He was putting this world together. Why is that important? Because knowing what He did right also gives you a clear understanding of what went wrong and what is wrong with the world. In my opinion, the book of Genesis is one of the most excellent writings of the Bible, if not one of *the* most important books.

It provides so much insight into humanity before and after the fall. Most of all, when I read and analyze this book, I can also see it from a parent's perspective. I can see God as a Father. A father who embodied so much love that He created a whole world for children to live and thrive in. A world designed to have and to give purpose. With everything being as perfect as it was, I know most have asked, "why in the world would God put the tree of knowledge of good and evil in the Garden knowing full well it would lead to their demise?"

My response to this age-old question is, "God was not in the business of designing robots." If you have read the entire first two chapters of Genesis, and you take a moment to look around the world that surrounds you, you will notice that God is extraordinarily detailed and creative. There are parts of this earth and universe that have yet to be explored. Why would a Creator with these amazing imaginative abilities create two people in His image and likeness that can't plan nor decide how they want to live? Why would he create children that would not be able to judge what is right versus what isn't? In short, God wanted humanity always to have the power of choice. The Garden was perfect, and the ability for man to choose was also perfection--it made them complete. To be able to choose gives one power. The power of choice gives way to freedom. Freedom allows life to grow and thrive, which was what God wanted since the very beginning, for both Adam and Eve to be fruitful and multiply.

The world they lived in came with all the beauty that a parent would want for their children. He creates Adam first and blesses his son with Eve. The gift of Eve to Adam was God creating an opportunity not only to have just one child but for them to birth many. Like any good father who symbolically gives their daughter's hand in marriage, they do so with the hope that the person their daughter is going to marry will love, provide, and protect her. God, already knowing what he placed in Adam, didn't hesitate to present Eve. As any good father would, He gave them his blessing to grow in abundance, to have dominion, and to fill the earth. With everything on the planet made to be good, the blessings were given, and life was being lived, so what went wrong? Why did Eve choose to fall for the bait?

Going back to my first question, *"Imagine for a second what it must've been like to be born into a world made exclusively for a man...*" Well, for starters, it appears that Adam created first, already formed a relationship with God the Father as a son. Eve's arrival on the scene came sometime after the animals were named. From the outside looking in, this gave the Serpent a perspective needed to bring a level of discomfort and mistrust into Eve's heart. **"Did God really say" and "you will be like God knowing good and evil"** was the wedge the Serpent inserted between a Father and His daughter. As a result, she reacts in a defiant daughter type of way and chooses to eat the fruit. Like so many of us, Eve struggled with what most would call today, a "daddy issue." At that moment, the Serpent conveyed something she had never experienced before, the feeling of lack. Not only did it make her feel that she lacked something, but it also put God at the root of what she lacked. That statement, *'did God really say,'* made her believe that her Father was holding back from her. The Serpent was creating a feeling of void, and she accepted it, by filling the void with a fruit that it promised would make her be like God, lacking nothing. Eve taking a bite out of that fruit was her wanting to fill an imaginary hole the Serpent faulted her into believing she had. The greatest lie of the first century is the same lie many of us are still battling with to this present day.

MY REFLECTION:

Do you have a strained relationship with your father? How did that impact your years of childhood? How does it affect you today? If you had a great relationship with your father growing up, how did that make you a better woman? How did your relationship, or non-existent relationship with your father impact your interactions with men?

_____
_____
_____
_____
_____
_____
_____
_____
_____
_____
_____
_____
_____
_____
_____
_____

Casey Alexis

"Daddy issues" have long since been the standard phrase for little girls who grow into their womanhood struggling with abandonment issues and pain from an absentee or abusive father. Like Eve, those daddy issues typically lead to the most destructive behaviors. Some of us seek and yearn for love and acceptance from male counterparts, while others on the other side of the spectrum, act out in anger towards males. It all stems from one place, missing out on the pure love of a father. As a result, instead of embracing good relationships centered in love, provision, and protection, we respond in defiance, seeking and attracting the complete opposite.

I do believe the act of defiance is not purposeful-- it's a result of an emptiness that we attempt to fill, where any attention becomes good attention. The controlling, manipulative behaviors equate to an "I love you." The type of promiscuous behavior that any form of "love" will do. Or we become so bitter; we don't want the love of a man in any way, whether in relationship or friendship. And finally, we don't know how to love because we've never seen nor experienced love in its purest form.

The void of a father's love leaves us susceptible to serpents like the Serpent who studied Eve so much, so; it knew that line, "did God really say," would work. At one time or another, we've all come across some "serpents" in human clothing. They can sniff out a woman that has daddy issues like a lion who preys on an injured animal. Daddy-daughter issues are gateways for predators who look to take advantage of childhood wounds and growing pains.

It is essential to know that you can heal from that hurt. To do that, it starts with forgiving your father for his absence and what his absence did to you. The forgiveness does not give him a pass, but it gives you the freedom you deserve to receive the love from a Father you always wanted. The love from God is a love that has a plan for you, a plan not to harm you, but a plan to give you hope and a future. It leads you to the truth that you no longer need to live to please others so they can stay. No longer will you do for others, because you need their love in return. No longer will you be a vessel to be used for pleasure so you can feel wanted. Finally, you will embrace life without carrying past hurts, and the abandonment once felt.

The daddy-daughter struggle is real. The feeling of abandonment is real. The lack of trust is real. These issues, plaguing the hearts of women all around the world, who seek the love of the father they never really had is real. Love in its purest form teaches us how we should be treated, cared for, protected, and uplifted in every way, and when that love is absent, it leaves a void. But one thing is for sure: filling that void with fake love is not it, it reaps counterfeit results. We've done that long enough, and it leads to further abandonment, deeper trust issues, and tons of hurt. Ladies, I am here to tell you there is hope. I've lived it, and I've come out on the other side; I know tons of women that have too.

As you will read on in the next few chapters, the love of the Father doesn't end because you missed out on the love from your earthly father. As we move forward, you will learn that a **REAL** Father's love can never separate him from his children, regardless of what they've done.

BEING EVE LESSON 3:

Believing the lies of the Serpent, brought a separation between me and God. The disconnect that was formed within that moment brought a wedge that made me feel devalued, as a result it changed my behavior which ultimately decreased what I felt I was worth.

But God... in all His goodness and the love He embodies as a Father, did not let the story of Adam and Eve fall into ruin after their choice was made. Even amid the greatest divide between God and man, His love did not and could not separate Him from His children. **(Romans 8:39)**

Being Eve in Adam's World

CHAPTER 4

THE REALITY OF IT ALL

By this time, Adam and Eve have both eaten the fruit, their perspectives have changed, things appear to be different, and eventually, they will meet with their Creator. Things are about to change, whether they fully understand it or not. I can only imagine the feelings that rushed through them with their new knowledge. I'm sure we can all relate to what they must have felt, precisely at a time in our lives when we've disobeyed our parents, and as a result, we sat in complete fear awaiting their return to dish out the punishment. Well, in **Genesis 3:7,** the scene begins with their eyes opened to a change in environment, a realization that they are naked, and a great need to cover up. As discussed in previous chapters, Eve was to Adam what Adam was to the Earth. Naturally, what transpired in Eve internally was revealed through Adam externally. After Adam ate the fruit, the Earth and everything in it changed.

The changes that took place in Eve compared to what took place when Adam ate of the fruit reveals many truths to the value and purpose of men and women in society. There are plenty of misconceptions and debates about what a man can do versus what a woman can do. And to be completely honest, the discussion is a waste of time. Roles are not meaningful if those who are operating in those assigned roles are ineffective. When Adam was created, God had a specific plan and purpose for him. That plan and purpose were for him to subdue and have dominion in maintaining the Earth. That plan and purpose did not change when Adam fell. He turned, and therefore the Earth changed with him, creating an atmosphere that would be difficult for Adam and his descendants to maintain. The same was for Eve; the purpose and plan God gave her to sustain life by being the Mother of all things living did not change. She changed, and therefore life born through her would be met with hardship for her and her descendants. We need to grab hold of this truth: although Adam and Eve changed, their roles didn't. Everything they were purposed to do, they still did, it was just met with extreme hardship as we will discover later in the book.

I know we are in the 21st century, and gender roles are under construction, but what's the real issue with the gender war? I believe the real problem with gender roles and the inequality experienced on both sides boils down to value. People lack the understanding of the importance of these roles within our foundational structure. When society devalues the purposes of either the man or the woman, it is because we lack knowledge of what those roles, in whatever capacity they are serving, have on the fragment of society. When you devalue something, you depreciate it, causing resentment in the heart of the person occupying the role. So, instead of being what we are in all fullness and glory, we desire to be something else that may appear to be of higher value. Historically a woman's worth stemmed from the value men placed on it. And that has indeed been our downfall since the beginning of The Fall. But we will get into that much later.

What resulted when Eve ate of the fruit compared to what happened when Adam ate of it was a startling difference. When Adam ate, everything on the Earth turned upside down.

When God created Adam, He created him from the Earth. Therefore, anything that transpired through Adam changed the environment. The same remains true for all of Adam's male descendants. This truth also applies to the descendants of Eve; therefore, anything that transpired through life, affected all life. It reveals a startling reality about the positions we play in the roles we occupy. I've learned that a life that is thriving versus a life that is not is entirely dependent on whether the environment where that life fills is appropriately maintained. And whether the conditions of that environment provide the sustenance required for that life to thrive. Just as God declared to Adam, subdue and have dominion and to the woman, be fruitful and multiply. Adam's choices will always provide the course of an environment. Eve's decisions will always be the gateway for life within that environment. Just like we discussed in the first chapter of this book, God designed this order so that both man and woman would intricately work together, sustaining, and maintaining life on Earth. This order also holds them liable to each other regarding the way they choose to live in their union.

You may be saying to yourself, *gosh Casey; this sounds very old fashioned.* Well, let me enlighten you just a bit. God sees gender roles quite differently than we do. His design and order were put into place so that ALL who occupied the Earth would thrive. Not a select population, not an elite group, not a select few, but *ALL*. Therefore because of the "*ALL*" factor, it is essential to note that we as humans don't think "*ALL,*" we think "*I,*" which is a big part of the problem. We don't often think of what is good for the collective; we believe what is right for ME, which is why half of the marriages today end in divorce. When God made man and woman, He designed them to intricately operate as a collective, one impacting the other so much so that the two become one. The "*I*" *is supposed to* turn into "*We,*" but as humans, we have a tough time letting go of that "*I.*"

For all my single ladies, you must understand this order that God put in place, and you must keep this in mind when you are deciding on the man you want to marry. If his choices create your environment, ladies choose wisely! Your environment ultimately creates your world, and your world dictates how well you thrive. If you place life in the hands of a man that has no clue how to maintain an environment for both of you to succeed in, you will suffer, and you will not be able to be effective in your role. It is also true for men. If a man chooses a woman to marry that harbors the qualities of death rather than life, his ability to have dominion, to subdue, and to maintain an environment that thrives will be near to impossible. When you understand God's original intent, you will make better choices, and you will also understand what is required of you to be productive, prosperous, and bountiful in it.

The person you decide to marry will be the most crucial decision you will ever make, and it will impact your entire life. Choose wisely, settle down with the person that you believe understands the roles, and the importance of you both operating intricately, as God designed. It is so important to follow the statutes that He put in place. "What God has joined together, let no man separate," that's the bible. So, let Him join you together. Don't force it because you've been dating for a while. Don't force it because you are feeling the pressure of society and parental figures regarding your age. Don't force marriage, period! Let God do the matchmaking, and all you have to do is follow the plan He already laid out since the very beginning.

Please understand labels created by men do not define the roles themselves. You can be in a marriage where the husband is more hospitable than the wife. You may see a union where the woman is better at managing finances than her husband. The importance of understanding God's intent to have the man as the maintainer, and the woman as the sustainer--I hope that you know, no one is greater, and no one is less. So, for example, in my home, my husband is great with hospitality. Everyone that knows us personally is fully aware that hospitality isn't one of my strengths. Still, as the maintainer of the environment, when he is doing what he is excellent at, it creates an environment that stimulates growth for everyone in it. With me, I am better with finances, so when I am doing what I am great at, we can thrive financially, which allows for everyone in our home to be sustained, and as a result, we thrive. Therefore, don't get caught up with labels of what one should be doing versus the other. Every relationship has its purpose, and we all have our core strengths. Be more concerned that you are competent in your roles as a maintainer (man) or a sustainer (woman).

With all of that noted, how does life in your housework? Are all living things in your home thriving? That's not a weird question to ask when you realize living things characterized as the living are growing, developing, moving, responding, adapting, evolving, and multiplying. Anything living in our homes that are not held by physical or mental limitations should be living as characterized. If they are not, we must be willing to do the necessary internal work to find out if there is anything in us that is a blockage to growth in our lives and our home.

Let me share a quick story of how this became so real in my own life. For many years, I had issues with keeping plants alive, and because of that, I never bought them. When my family and I finally moved to Georgia, I decided to purchase a house plant I was familiar with; I saw my mother take outstanding care of a similar plant for many years. As you can probably imagine, I never really cared for the plant. It had gotten so bad that my mom visited and resurrected the plant for me. A little while after she left, the poor plant began to dwindle again. I didn't know what to do, but I didn't want to kill the darn thing! So, the next best thing I thought of was to place it outside on the patio and hope that being in its natural environment, the plant would persevere. Well, eventually it did, but as the season changed from summer to fall, the plant began to change too.

In 2018, when I began working on this book, God began to work on my heart regarding the plant. A conviction came over me as I stared at the plant from the inside of my home. From the inside looking out, the plant appeared to be freezing. My heart began to speak, and I could hear it say, "how could I have the gift to create and stimulate life, but yet, I can't care for a plant?" So, I took the plant from the patio, and I began to love it by speaking life into it every day. I watered it, and at times, talked to its leaves. My daughters have also grown to show love to it, and presently, my husband loves it as well. Inevitably, God used that opportunity to teach me that as women, we can transfer life or death to every living thing in our home and not even be aware of it.

Now that our marriage is thriving, and so is the plant, it got me thinking about why I purchased it in the first place, knowing all too well I don't do well with plants. At the time, I bought the plant with a hope that because we were in a new environment (moving from Massachusetts to Georgia), my heart set to take care of it. But I soon realized after we settled in that our family changed locations, but our dynamics were still the same, and so the environment was still toxic in our home. Our sites changed, but the marriage was still a mess, and so was the situation in the house. As a result, I remained the same, which meant the plant's survival rate was little to non-existent. I had held onto this hope that the new location would provide a new environment; I soon learned that was not the case.

My spouse and I have been through a lot within our 13 years of marriage, and as I reflect on the truth of how God designed the relationship between man and woman, I understand why it was a never-ending cycle of hurt. We were intricately working together unknowingly feeding death into our environment and our lives. Like most, when we got married, we had no clue what we were doing or what we were getting ourselves into. We were in love, we were exclusive for about five years, and naturally, we believed that we were ready for marriage. We were so wrong! Neither of us understood our roles. We didn't understand the way God designed this thing to work. After experiencing loss, heartache, hatred, betrayal, and eventually a yearlong separation, we finally sought the therapy we both so desperately needed. We realized if we didn't heal, we would never be able to create the environment we so desperately wanted but just didn't know how to maintain or sustain it. After getting the help we needed, which opened our eyes to a whole lot, we understood that we were once ***the walking dead.*** We were in a dead marriage, barely surviving in a dead environment, and if we didn't get it together, the children that we finally did have would fight for their lives trying to become thriving adults.

MY REFLECTION:

(SINGLE LADIES):

Do you believe you are ready for marriage? Are you thriving? Do you currently care for anything that is living? Is that living thing you are caring for thriving? What type of environment do you believe will be conducive to your growth? If you desire to be married, what are you doing to prepare for your role in the marriage?

_____
_____
_____
_____
_____
_____
_____
_____
_____
_____
_____
_____
_____
_____
_____
_____

MY REFLECTION:

(MARRIED LADIES):

Are you living a life that thrives? Is the living thing you are responsible for thriving? Is your environment conducive to living things? As a couple, are you intricately working together for the greater good of all who live in the home?

_____
_____
_____
_____
_____
_____
_____
_____
_____
_____
_____
_____
_____
_____
_____
_____
_____

The reality of it all is that life after The Fall, is a big mess and because of the imperfections, it is essential for us to understand that we will have transitions, failures, and lessons. The key to it all is understanding. Understanding who we are, our purpose, what our roles are in the home, and finally understanding each other. In this way, in our positions, we can equally hold each other accountable when things are not operating in the home as they should. At this point, I would like to insert some interesting facts. Currently, the divorce rate with the millennial generation (my generation) is decreasing because we are waiting longer to get married and, as a result, are staying married longer. I do believe it is due to the flexibility we have with our roles.

We are learning not to allow the labels created by man to dictate our homes, which would enable us to be great in the positions we hold, and hopefully operate to the maximum capacity. I would also like to take the time to point out that the divorce rates of those who have divorced and remarried a 2nd or 3rd time are significantly higher. So, if you don't understand what your role is the first time, and you don't do the necessary work from within to heal and find that out. You won't learn it with a second or a third person. Save yourself the trouble and do the work, so when you do meet the person God has set aside for you to do life with, you both will thrive!

So, as we end this chapter on the realness of marriage and all that it entails, Adam and Eve didn't have a clue of what their new reality had in store for them. It all became real as they transitioned from a life of abundance to something else; they did not know. In a moment after eating the fruit, they both awakened to their new-found life. The first thing they were aware of was their appearance. They realized they were naked, and therefore found a need to find a place to hide. What was once befitting became shame.

They heard God approaching, and just like children who know when they have done wrong, they hid. God called out to Adam first, most likely knowing something was awry with the environment. Adam responded, *"I heard you in the Garden, and I was afraid because I was naked; so, I hid."* His response confirmed what God already knew. They had indeed eaten from the tree. Adam's reaction filled with fear and shame--two emotions never intended for humanity to know. How could anyone maintain a healthy, thriving environment living in fear and shame? So, the question arose, **"who told you that you were naked?"**

Being Eve Lesson 4:

Adam and I were one when we were formed by God, and when we disobeyed God we fell as one.

In a marriage, typically there is a lot of compromising. Sometimes it's balanced between the couple, and often one person does more compromising than the other. Either way, in order to be effective in whatever you are doing, agreement is required. So, if your environment and your lives are not thriving, both man and woman must take a very close look at themselves because you are both equally responsible for the outcomes. Can two people walk together without agreeing on the direction? **(Amos 3:3)**

Casey Alexis

CHAPTER 5

THE BLAME GAME & THE SCAPEGOAT

The initial question *"who told you that you were naked?"* was the beginning of the very first blame game ever recorded in biblical history. God continued, *"have you eaten from the tree that I commanded you not to eat from?"* Adam's response to God immediately blames Eve. Although the fruit did come from Eve's hand, God asked him specifically if he ate from the tree? His response could have simply been, *"yes...I did eat from the tree."* However, with fear and shame in the mix, Adam chose not to place himself at the feet of responsibility. Instead, he decided on a scapegoat.

The scapegoat was none other than Eve. What was taken from his side was now used as an attempt to shield him from his consequences. What Adam did is a perfect example of what occurs when some men fear straight into failure, by not dealing with their insecurities, faults, and issues. Instead, they choose a scapegoat, and often, it is someone in their sphere of influence. In Adam's case, it was his wife. The improper use of the woman's purpose was a direct result. When a man uses a woman as a scapegoat, she becomes a source of life to drain to shield him from his consequences of dealing with himself, his insecurities, fears, faults, and issues.

Revisiting Chapter 2, we understand that a woman's gift is in her ability to provide life to everything around her. A man who understands this well can do two things: He will encourage it, so not only does he thrive, but he maintains an environment where she thrives, and as a result, everyone who resides in that environment also thrives. Or on the other hand, he can decide to use the woman selfishly to be his scapegoat, his resource. Using the woman as an attempt to fill the voids in his life, a void she can never fill. Typically, this occurs through sexual activity or an ongoing unhealthy relationship.

He will take from the woman, draining her until she has nothing left to give, or until she understands her value and releases herself. In the worst-case scenarios, he will tap multiple women simultaneously, never maintaining life by providing a suitable environment for any of them. As a result, he takes, and he goes. In some of these cases, he will produce life and leave the woman with the fruit of her womb, abandoned in a world where they will have hardship. Often left with the burden to raise a child or children alone, or even worse, to decide whether she wants to continue with the pregnancy. Fostering an environment of survival, forced to change her true nature of nurturer and protector into that which is the complete opposite. Understand this--women who are living in thriving environments aren't typically the ones who consider aborting a child. They usually have the support required. Unlike the woman who is the scapegoat, she is unaware of her value and has never truly experienced an environment that fostered her growth. The thought of bringing a life into an already harmful environment can be very disheartening.

As the ongoing battle between the Right to Life versus the Pro-Choice movement rages, I encourage both sides to understand this perspective. A woman doesn't necessarily **want** to choose to end a pregnancy. That would be against her nature. Most of the time, her options of creating a healthy environment for that child seem so bleak, and the odds she believes are already set against her seem so high, in her mind, she thinks it's her ***only*** option. I challenge both sides to operate with some grace. Don't judge too harshly at what some may feel it is the only option they have at that moment. The God-given authority to be a great mother to sustain a loving and nurturing environment that fosters growth will seem like a difficult task when done alone, and it is. Especially if you've never seen it for yourself and don't believe you can provide it. In those circumstances, I can understand why the tree of knowledge of good and evil can and will sound a little louder than the tree of life. I stood at both trees when I was eighteen years old. I was afraid, and I didn't know what to do. In my mind, the only option was to hide in shame and to rid myself of the guilt quickly and quietly. I made a choice to eat from the tree of knowledge of good and evil, and it wasn't because I wanted it--I just lacked so much at the time, and I didn't think life was even an option. I wish back then someone would have told me what I am about to say to you.

If you are currently struggling with this choice as you read this book, or if you ever decided to end your pregnancy, please know this: GOD LOVES YOU. The option is and never was easy to make. If you are currently struggling with this decision, I will tell you this: Don't let your current circumstances dictate the future. You are and always will be a giver of life. The environment you decide to bring your child in will thrive if you make the conscious effort to do it. It won't be easy, but it is worth it. And it can be done as many women continue to do it daily on their own. And if you decide you can't do it on your own, there are other options. Many women all around the world have thriving environments that are eager to provide that to your unborn child. I would be remiss as a woman who's been through this heart-wrenching decision not to be honest with you. I know all too well that the hurt and shame doesn't go away after the procedure. There's a whole heap of mental, emotional, and spiritual consequences that most don't speak about when dealing with the aftermath of an abortion. I would be remiss to be who I am today and not encourage you to choose life. Choose life because it is in your very nature to fight to live. Give your child that chance.

Lastly, the Serpent in the Garden hasn't changed his skin. It is the same Serpent today. Urging us all to the question, did God *really* say to be fruitful and multiply? Its aim has always been to kill, steal, and destroy. We are deliberately manipulated to believe a lie rather than the truth, so we can doubt God and begin to look at our children as burdens rather than blessings. And on the other end, we know the aim of God has and will continue to be to choose LIFE. When we make the distinct decision to go against what God has decreed, it is to commit a crime against the very thing He's called and created us to do. How so? Well, the bible says, "every good and perfect gift comes from God." So when we take matters into our own hands to shed the blood of the innocent, we are held accountable.

What saved me and prayerfully what will save you is knowing, trusting, and believing in the redemption of our sins (we will get into more of that later). God is ready and willing to be a father to your fatherless child, to help and support you to raise that baby by sending willing servants to be His hands and feet. Trust God and choose life!

If you made the mistake that I did and entertained the words of the Serpent against life, there is hope and salvation for you that no man can give. God is our refuge and our strength. He promises the forgiveness of our sins through repentance, much like when He told the Serpent that the woman would bear an offspring that will crush his head. In the same way, the promise of vengeance and reconciliation is unadulterated. So, I urge you as you read, if your heart is still troubled about your decision on that day, God is able. Repent, ask for forgiveness. God will make you whole again. The memory won't ever go away, but I promise you, He will heal your heart, and you will regain a newfound understanding that He will use for His glory. But first, you must accept responsibility for your decisions and not cast blame.

The blame game would have us believe that if we dump the consequences of our decisions from one person to another, we won't have to take responsibility for our actions. The man leaving you on your own to carry the decision and the burden of choosing life or death for your unborn is him not taking responsibility for his actions. A woman now left to bear that blame then puts it on the unborn child who never gets a chance to live out their life. The blame game is a never-ending cycle of trying to escape one's consequences when, in reality, one will never be able to avoid what is rightfully theirs.

For those of us who are married or in committed relationships, I can boldly attest that we all have probably experienced the blame game at least once. Can I get an AMEN? Contrary to what some may believe, there's not much of a difference in a man's actions when he is in a committed relationship, struggling to deal with his insecurities, faults, and issues. He will more than likely operate in the same fashion, draining his wife while providing an unsuitable, never consistent, dysfunctional environment. In these cases, the wife will often take on additional responsibilities she was not designed for, hoping to offer some form of resolution, especially if there are children involved. As a result, she is often very weary, tired, and overwhelmed, attempting to be both the sustainer and the maintainer in the home.

Being both can seem like her best option of survival, being a covering for his insecurities, managing his faults, and attempting to console all his issues does the complete opposite. Wives, when you become the "covering" for your spouse, you are mainly covering up and hiding the mess. You are stepping in as a scapegoat. You are now willingly taking his confusion, his load, and wearing it on your back. The survival you are hoping for is not survival at all. It is a slow, agonizing journey, filled with rough terrain. It is a terrain you were not designed for because that is not what you were purposed for. To be completely honest, the only thing you are doing is preventing God from doing His best work. God uses the rough terrain to deal with your spouse to shape and mold him, just like when He shaped and molded Adam from the earth. God subsequently breathed life into him from that process. When you step in as a scapegoat, you prevent God from using that terrain to shape and mold him, and therefore the man will never be fashioned into the man He called him to be. As we get further into the book and the consequences of Adam eating the fruit, you will come to understand why this truth is so imperative.

As the blame game ensues and moved from Adam to Eve, she followed suit and placed the blame on the Serpent. Although the Serpent did deceive her, it did not force her to eat. Her decision was hers and hers alone. The choice to eat was also hers and hers alone. Eve did what so many of us women often do when we fail to take responsibility for our actions. We move to place the blame on everything else living, but ourselves. We will quickly blame other women because of our insecurities, or we will blame men for the things they aren't doing, while we often aren't doing what we have been called to do. Some of us find ourselves even blaming our children, tearing through them with our words, provoking them with our anger, and demeaning them because of our bitterness.

As a result, those of us who fall for the blame game will more than likely find it challenging to maintain healthy relationships. Friendships will be baseless, connections will be unfruitful, and kids often unhappy. Fruit from the tree of knowledge of good and evil are the only fruits they will often share. They are the women the Bible speaks of who tear down their homes with their bare hands (Proverbs 14:1) -- Never truly allowing anything in their environment to thrive, even if their spouse is a great maintainer. Nothing truly succeeds because the woman operates far too frequently from a place of death. Unfortunately, playing the blame game as Eve did is often a more natural pill to swallow rather than looking in the mirror to face ourselves. As a result, we never really own up to the fact that we must take responsibility for our decisions and the consequences to follow.

MY REFLECTION:

Have you ever played the blame game? Do you look at your actions prior to reviewing the actions of others? How prone are you to accept responsibility for your own personal failures?

The blame game is not useful for the way God designed the man and woman to work so intricately together. Just like Adam and Eve were held responsible for their own set of consequences, it is the same with us who are in a relationship. Each of us should be ready and willing to be held responsible for our role in building or destroying our environments.

The blame game eventually came to an end after Eve blamed the serpent, but what ushered in immediately afterward was conviction and correction. You see, the result of the blame game was the refusal to accept responsibility. To God, that was a clear sign of unrepentance. When an individual is not remorseful, there is no room for restoration to the original relationship. How can you truly move forward in a relationship when a person decides not to accept their responsibility for the fallout? What happened next truly changed the dynamics of Adam and Eve's relationship with each other and their relationship with God. The change was so shattering that it impacts the world to this very day.

BEING EVE LESSON 5:

It was so easy to blame Adam for my decision just as much as it was for him to pass blame onto me. But we were both responsible. Maybe if we had just confessed to our wrong-doing things could have been different.

Adam and Eve was desperately looking for a scapegoat to carry the burden of their disobedience. Unfortunately, because they were all guilty, no single person or thing could carry out the verdict they received. The blame game doesn't serve anyone when we all have sinned and fallen short of the glory of God. But God, in His infinite mercy, had a rescue plan. **(1 Peter 2:22-25)**

Being Eve in Adam's World

CHAPTER 6

THE END OF A FAIRYTALE

When Adam first laid eyes on Eve; he was in awe. He referred to her as the **"flesh of my flesh and bone of my bone,"** but after the fall, she became **"the woman you gave me."** My, my, my how things have changed. The tree of knowledge of good and evil not only changed them, but it also distorted their perspective. What once was good and pleasing to the eye quickly became their shame. Being naked was no longer acceptable; the moment they ate, they looked to be covered—the Serpent who was once agreeable to listen to became a deceiver. The woman Adam once looked upon in awe, became the sole reason behind his fall. The freedom they once had to walk and talk with God turned into fear once the presence of God was near. And just like that, the fairytale turned into a thriller, and they were no longer the same.

In **Genesis 3:14**, the time had arrived for God to speak and dish out some consequences. He'd heard the failed attempts of blame from both Adam and Eve. Their failure to accept responsibility for their actions, repent and therefore be restored, left God in a place where conviction and correction were the means of recourse. In Chapter 3, I discussed God being a parent who created a perfect environment that His children would be able to live and thrive in. The guidelines set in that environment were to encourage their growth. Unfortunately, eating the fruit changed them entirely, making them no longer suitable to remain in the condition that God originally put in place. Because of that, things needed to change, new guidelines were required, and God did just that.

First up was the Serpent, the one who caused the deception. God placed a curse upon the Serpent that not only changed its position, but its mobility, its functionality, and most importantly, its role between the woman and her descendants. The Serpent lost its status and its access. To come and to go as it pleased now came with some difficulty. It also gained what would be a long-standing battle between Eve, her children, and the offspring of the Serpent. God was also clear to mention that one of Eve's descendants would crush the Serpent's head, destroying it once and for all. The Serpent is the antagonist in the story symbolic of the role of God's eternal enemy, Satan. Without going into the depths of his biblical story, Satan, famously known as Lucifer, has been an enemy of God before the creation of man. He has always desired to be like God and to rule like God. This desire was his downfall, and he aimed to ensure it became the downfall of humanity.

Satan's role in the deception of man was to destroy what God loves the most, by destroying what He created through humanity. The methods used by Satan have been consistent throughout biblical history; deception will and always be his end game. His ability to distort the truth, causing doubt, fear, and unbelief, has been his go-to approach. Unfortunately, to this very day, humanity struggles to find a clear path of love, justice, and peace, due to this perpetual cycle of distortion of what God truly intended when he created the earth and its inhabitants. More on this later, but I wanted to highlight the reason behind the Serpent's deception and the importance of understanding why he came for Adam and Eve in the Garden.

After God finished with the Serpent, it was Eve's turn. Her role in being fruitful and multiplying didn't change, but with it would come with some pain. God told her she would experience a significant increase in pain with childbearing. When I read this, I immediately began to question, *well, what happens to women who never experience the pain of bearing an actual child?* Then it came to me. **Bringing life into the world is not confined to only birthing a human being.** The act of giving life also falls under birthing dreams, ideas, businesses, and even relationships. The process and the pain associated with seeing those things become a reality can surely be relative to the trimesters of carrying and birthing an actual child. As women, we are known to try our best to withstand pain long enough in the hopes of attaining a living, breathing, healthy reward in the end. However, in all instances where it takes two to tango, the condition of that desire is never truly in our hands alone. Specifically, when it depends heavily on the environment, we are a part of, and whether those who occupy the environment are effective in their roles. This is not a strange thought when you think of a woman trying to grow and be a success in an unhealthy relationship or a toxic environment.

Therefore, it is essential to understand the way God designed life to work. The more you know, the less inclined you'll be to hold onto or wait out for a great birthing experience knowing specific environments will not be conducive for growth--especially if a critical role player doesn't want to do the necessary work to change. Again, this should help you to be more mindful of the Adams and the Eves you choose to have in your life. If the Adam you love, or the Adam you work alongside, or the Adam's you surround yourself with are terrible maintainers, your chances of success are incredibly minimal. You will carry their burdens and never truly walk away with an entirely happy, healthy, living reward at the end. The same applies to a woman who is in a leadership capacity but is a terrible sustainer in her role; any other woman or man associated with her in any size will have a hard time with growth. Trust me, -- been there, done that, and I am sure if you think about it, you have too.

With that noted, it leads me straight into the next consequence given to Eve that, most women, have been contending with for many generations. God told Eve, **"your desire will be for your husband, and he will rule over you."** Those words are a significant blow because it made Eve subservient to Adam. It hurt me just to type that, *but it's true.* Her deception led to the betrayal of Adam, which caused a significant shift on earth and a continued downward spiral within humanity. Her husband is ruling over her, resulting in her being under his authority. It also caused her to operate in a space where she hadn't been before. Instead of being by his side, she was now behind him. I know we are centuries away from what transpired, but this is the experience of all women today. Despite what that great Beyoncé anthem may tell you, girls we *DON'T* run the world. We have been contending with this fact for a very long time, and I am here to shine a bright light on why it's true.

I know many of you would probably argue with me because of all the changes from a gender perspective. Yes, there's no doubt about it, women have made some fantastic contributions to society, and we have come a long way compared to past generations. However, if you take a moment and look past the surface level, you will realize at the root of it all, the contentious battle to overrule the rulership of the man has been misleading. The response of the women's rights movement and every feminist movement came from our desire to attain equality with our male counterparts. The root of our desires always stems from what men do. As a result, we are still responding. We are never leading. The movements were birthed out of reaction, not out of purpose, which explains why some of these movements are rooted in anger, revenge, bitterness, dishonor, and death to patriarchy disguised as empowerment.

The movements are a battle cry for restoration to the place we once held, but instead of aligning with our Creator and finding our true purpose, we continue to allow creation to dictate our course of action. We continue to make the mistake Eve made when she let the serpent deceptively coarse her into action by eating the fruit. I genuinely believe this is where we often lose because our innate characteristics are to embody and give life in everything that we do. In turn, the deconstruction of the role of men in society to empower us is an oxymoron. It is not to our benefit to react in hopes of destroying a patriarchal system to stir everyone into a matriarchal system. But to lead with purpose and align with our male counterparts to create a better future together. Understand this--You cannot put down one to exalt the other and expect true empowerment and prosperity. The roles of both the man (maintainer) and the woman (sustainer) are equally crucial to the overall success of humanity.

MY REFLECTION:

Have you ever experienced consequences that changed your life? Did those changes have a negative or a positive impact on you?

As we move from the consequences of Eve and stroll right into Adam's, we learned that God cursed the earth, causing Adam to work hard to maintain the earth from where he was formed. God cursed the ground, life on Earth has drastically changed, and physical death is now imminent. Adam was told he would work hard for everything he needs, and he will sweat while doing it. Hardship is now a part of their roles and has now become a massive part of their journey.

Adam and Eve have both transitioned into new lives doing what they were purposed to do, but now it comes with the knowledge of good and evil. They've transitioned from a place of authority and divinity to what we now call human. God selected conviction and correction as a path for them to endure the pain in their roles-- Giving them the understanding of their mistake, but also the need to understand the harsh reality of their disobedience. It created a space, a hunger, and a need for a savior to rescue them.

After they both received their consequences, God puts them out of the Garden, ending all access to the tree of life, causing them to live under the fallen condition. Even with the consequences and the relocation, being the good Father that He is, God doesn't leave them exposed and in their shame. God gives them a promise of hope through the birth of more children, a child that will redeem them from their fall. He covers them with clothes and sends them out of the Garden to live out their remaining years.

> ## BEING EVE LESSON 6:
>
> ### My actions changed everything...
>
> It is important to remember that one action can cause several chain reactions that you may not be ready for. Thankfully, God's grace is bigger than our mistakes and although we will still go through our consequences, he is faithful enough to carry us and provide a way through. **(1 Peter 5:10)**

CASEY ALEXIS

CHAPTER 7

THE PRESENT CHANGES THE FUTURE

Adam and Eve lived for quite some time after The Fall. The Bible references Adam living for 930 years. In that time, life outside of the Garden was as God described. Human nature was now at the forefront, replacing what was known to them as perfection. Adam worked by the sweat of his brow, and Eve would travail in laboring children. Beginning in **Genesis 4**, the Bible goes on to introduce their two sons, the first-named Cain and the other named Abel, both born after The Fall. I am sure when Eve had her boys, she was filled with joy-- like any mother would be. She was bringing life into the world, and who knows, she may have even thought to herself, *"perhaps one of them will be the one who will crush the head of the Serpent as foretold by God."* Maybe she hoped that such occurrences would allow her to attain vengeance against the Serpent and hopefully restore them to the Garden.

As the chapter continues, we learn that both Cain and Abel, like their parents, had distinct responsibilities. One was the keeper of the soil (earth), producing fruits, and the other was the keeper of the animals (life). God would continue to visit them at this time, and each one would bring him an offering based upon what they were responsible for. As you can probably imagine, this was more than likely a high-pressure situation. They would want to make sure God received the best of the best, right? Well, Cain decided to bring God what he was comfortable with, while Abel chose to bring God more than his best-- he brought *the best.* Isn't it interesting that the one who took care of life, brought the best gift, while the other who was responsible for the fruit brought what he felt was the best? It's very reminiscent of the decision Adam and Eve had to make in the Garden. Because Abel made the right decision, God showed him favor.

As any parent would, you reward your child when they do the right things. Unfortunately, in a world that is fallen, openly rewarding, someone can bring jealousy to the hearts of those who decide to live in mediocrity. The favor that God displayed towards Abel brewed jealousy in Cain, and God took notice. Knowing full well what man has become, God tells Cain to fight the urge against the fallen human nature, reminding him that it doesn't have any control over him unless he lets it. Cain, like his parents, had a decision to make: Symbolically, he could either eat from the tree of life or he could eat from the tree of knowledge of good and evil. If you are not familiar with this part of the story, spoiler alert, Cain decides to deceive his brother and kills him. He takes a big 'ole bite of the fruit on the tree of knowledge of good and evil.

Just when you thought things couldn't get worse, the very worst occurs. A life was taken-- the consequence of eating the fruit from the tree of knowledge of good and evil has presented itself in the next generation. The Bible doesn't speak on Adam and Eve's reaction or involvement. I believe this is due to focusing the reader on God's relationship with the next generation. It was also an opportunity to give a raw example regarding the aftermath of eating the fruit. It provided a look into how the human condition would look like going forward.

Eve's reaction, not mentioned, but as a mother, I can only imagine what she may have been feeling at this point. I'm sure she had A broken heart, deep anguish, confusion, and a sense of dismay that her child took the life of his brother. I am sure she also probably battled with guilt, thinking about how her decision in the Garden led to the death of her son. She more than likely replayed the conversation she had with the Serpent in her mind a thousand times, questioning what she could have done differently. She probably dreamt about the life they all would have had if she had denied the fruit. Possibly dwelling on the hope deferred that at least one child would crush the head of the Serpent. At this point, I am sure the blame game became a recurring factor. She could have possibly blamed Adam for whatever he did or didn't do to teach the boys about honoring God with their best gifts, and loving each other as brothers, etc. I am sure they argued about it, hurt about it, cried about it, and eventually, they healed through it.

A loss for any woman is painful. I remember the first time I lost a child through an early miscarriage; it was so traumatic. I never had the chance to hold the child, feel its breath, or even hear its heartbeat, but the pain was as high as if I had known that child its entire life. I opted out of a D&C for several reasons, so I felt the pain of labor as my body naturally went through the process of miscarrying. I remember saying to myself, "*I am giving birth to death.*" It was the most difficult, heart-wrenching, an eye-opening experience I have ever undergone, and I wouldn't wish it on anyone. In normal circumstances, the connection that a woman has with her child is instant; there is an immediate need to protect, nurture, and love that child. So, I can only imagine the pain a woman carries when she has held a child, knowing every piece of that child down to their toes, and then the worst part of life happens; death comes and takes that child away. It's an unimaginable pain, and I am sure many of us have our own stories that can relate to Eve's loss, whether it was a loss through miscarriage, sickness, accident, or by violence. It's a loss, and it takes a piece of you with it.

I know some women struggle to have a viable pregnancy, and that too is a loss. It comes with an extreme amount of shame. I've also have been there. To this very day (well, at least until this book is made public), most of my family doesn't know that my husband and I suffered through not one, but three miscarriages before having both of our daughters. It's a shame that most of us women carry, not because someone places the guilt on us, but because we put it on ourselves. Although miscarriages happen quite frequently, distinctly, our instincts are fully aware that the ability to carry life is our superpower, and when something goes wrong, we feel broken.

MY REFLECTION:

Have you suffered a loss of a child? Did you blame yourself or someone close to you? How did you manage through life after the loss? Have you healed from that loss? Have you talked to anyone about your loss?

_____
_____
_____
_____
_____
_____
_____
_____
_____
_____
_____
_____
_____
_____
_____
_____
_____
_____

The feeling of brokenness does not only apply to those of us who have experienced a miscarriage. It also applies to those who cannot get pregnant at all. It is a burden that no woman should carry alone. I want you to know that you are loved, and countless women all around the world support and stand with you. We know the quiet shame you have endured. Shame no more, contrary to what you may feel. Your superpower goes beyond the ability to carry life-- it's also essential to sustain life. Think about it: there are plenty of women who can bring life, but they are unfit to care for and nurture that life. Being a life-bearer is much more than the ability to carry; we must also be willing to sustain life as well. You are not broken. You have plenty of experience to offer and love to give. I encourage us all to submit our life-giving nature to the world around us. We can achieve this through acts of service within our neighborhood, the local church, local organizations, fostering children, and adoption, etc. There is so much life you can offer. Spread life by touching lives.

And most importantly, support each other. There is no greater encouragement in the world, then another woman speaking life and encouraging life into another woman. The courage you feel when another woman supports you and uplifts you are an unstoppable force that pushes you forward into places that you never thought you would go. It's kind of crazy how we are the hardest on each other, yet in reality, we need one another. Most of what we go through is so similar in life, but the deception is to divide us so that we never truly understand how powerful we are together. Supporting one another and encouraging one another is a gift, and we should always use that gift to promote life within each other to do amazing things.

As we dive back into Eve's reality and look into Cain's journey, we learn that God eventually calls out to Cain, asking for his brother. According to his response, you can tell Cain didn't have much reverence for God, which was evident with his gift offering as well. His response was a lot different from Adam's reaction when he messed up. The moment Adam realized a change took place, he hid with the quickness! He was fearful and ashamed of himself, but Cain, on the other hand, was as bold as sin. It is a stark look into how life inside the Garden of Eden was very different from being outside of the Garden. The reverence of God had already begun to dissipate as Cain responds to God with a rhetorical question, "am I my brother's keeper?"

To that response, God tells him he knows of his brother's death, **"your brother's blood cries out to me from the ground (Genesis 4:10)."** Consequently, God marks him and then banishes him from the land of his family, sending him away. So, not only did Adam and Eve lose one son, but the experience took Cain too. I can only assume Eve's heart was not as conflicted with this loss due to Cain's transgression, but she would never see him again. The decision to eat from the tree of knowledge of good and evil was much more ruthless than imagined. The great deception the Serpent fed her about being just like God, was more than she ever bargained. I'm sure Eve didn't realize that knowing good would also come with a heap of knowing evil. She probably never imagined things like murder, heartbreak, death, and loss would be something she never thought she'd experience.

MY REFLECTION:

Have you ever done something and realized the consequences of that decision was something you had not bargained for? How did you handle that situation?

As we reflect, notice generations later us knowing evil is still one of the biggest hang-ups between man and God. Knowing sin is where most people struggle with, "If God exists, why do bad things happen to good people?" Here are my thoughts--we have a bunch of Cain's in this world, who have the choice to do good, but would instead do evil. Sometimes those choices negatively impact the Abel's of the world. Being born into a fallen world, we are left with decisions to make every single day. Some of those choices bring out the best in us, while others bring out the worst. Please understand that God still allows us the freedom to make those choices, and He also allows us to have dominion and to subdue. Remember, the only thing that changed was Adam and Eve, but their roles remained the same.

After the heartache, one thing I know for sure, Eve realized the desire to be like God wasn't what it's cracked up to be. It came with a load that Adam and Eve were not prepared to handle. It remains valid for all of us to this very day.

Being Eve Lesson 7

Consequences changes things. The fall of Adam and I created a world that was unknown to us. We had no idea the one decision to eat the fruit would lead to circumstances that would transcend time and continue hurt generations after us.

The moment we give into our temptations we open the door for consequences to follow. And oftentimes those consequences are much more than we bargained for. Unfortunately, life doesn't come with a reset button. Therefore, it so important to follow the guidelines provided to us, they will always be a light unto our feet and a light unto our path. **(Proverbs 14:12 / Psalm 119:105-106)**

CHAPTER 8

LIFE GOES ON

As we all know, whether from personal experience or a story of a loved one, tragedy can certainly impact our lives for a very long time. Let me be a reminder to you: it doesn't have to stop us from living, because it didn't stop Adam and Eve. For their sake and the earth, they were fruitful, they multiplied, and they occupied themselves, life had to go on. Well into their years, Adam and Eve ended up having another son and named him Seth. Eve's heart filled with joy, the bible says, *Genesis 4:25, "God has granted me another child in place of Abel since Cain killed him."* That verse lets me know that Eve still held onto hope despite all the mistakes. Although Abel was now gone and Cain banished, her ability to do the things she was purposed to do as the mother of all things living was a great reminder that God was not done with them yet. The promise given to them about an offspring that would crush the head of the Serpent was still possible; the dream to get back to the Garden was still alive. The Bible goes on to reveal that Adam and Eve had several additional children, and their children had children, and the story continues for many generations to this very day.

It's incredible what caring for another life can do to inspire us as women to keep hope alive and to continue the fight. In the time that I have written this book, I have spoken to countless women of different age groups and backgrounds. I've noticed that throughout our stories, there was a common thread. The moment we had children or cared for another life was when our hearts shifted to where we no longer settle for the bare minimum of what life was offering. We wanted to be examples of those we cared for and loved. We wanted them to see us thriving and not just surviving. The mere hope that if we succeeded, we would keep them from making the same mistakes was a fire underneath us. Like Eve, we wanted them to know that there was still hope in living.

Genesis 4:25 was Eve's last documented statement, and it ended with finding hope through tragedy. That verse encouraged me always to strive to be hopeful in all things. The tragedies I've suffered doesn't define my life story, and it shouldn't set yours. Remind yourself that your current circumstances should not and will not dictate your future self. We've all suffered through tragedy, some of them were more difficult than others, but they do not negate our purpose. We all have a mission; you still have a purpose! Tragedy may delay us, but it shouldn't define us, and it most certainly should not stop us from doing what we are purposed to do. If anything, our obstacles can be considered our qualifiers. The tragedies we overcome qualify us to go and speak in places others do not have the authority to go. For example, if you are a mother who lost a child through gun violence, and you've successfully been able to find hope through your tragedy, there is no one more qualified than you to speak to a group of mothers who are now where you used to be. If you are a victim of physical abuse, and you were able to heal through your tragedy, there is no one more qualified than you to speak to a group of people who are in a dark place and need to hear your story. It's time to remove the shackles of all the years of hurt and pain. It is time to allow them to become your story of hope for the future. Take your story back! Take your life back! Take that tragedy and breathe a new life into it! Change the narrative it thought it had over you. It will not be the end of your story. It will not define your story. Use it as a stepping stone to greatness.

MY REFLECTION:

What's your story? Write it down and share it with at least one person.

_____
_____
_____
_____
_____
_____
_____
_____
_____
_____
_____
_____
_____
_____
_____
_____
_____
_____
_____
_____
_____
_____

Genesis 4:25 was the last statement from Eve, and it was also the final written entry to her story. Still, her story continues to live on throughout the lives of her daughters, whose stories continued through the biblical pages of Genesis through to Revelation. From Sarah, wife of Abraham; Hagar, mother of Ishmael; Rebekah, wife of Isaac; Rachel, wife of Jacob; Leah, also wife of Jacob; Jochebed, mother of Moses; Rahab, the prostitute turned ancestor of King David and Jesus Christ; Deborah, the first female Judge of Israel; Ruth, a young widow became ancestor of King David and Jesus Christ; Hannah, mother of the Prophet Samuel; Bathsheba, mother of King Solomon; Esther, unknown Jewish girl turned Persian Queen; Elizabeth, mother of John the Baptist; Mary, the mother of Jesus Christ; Mary and Martha, sisters of Lazarus; Mary Magdalene, prostitute turned disciple of Jesus Christ; and all the countless women that supported Jesus and his disciples out of their own means; Lydia, one of the first converts after the death of Jesus Christ; Priscilla, disciple of Paul and follower of Jesus Christ; Phoebe, Deacon in the early church under Paul; Casey, woman of God and follower of Jesus Christ; **include YOUR NAME HERE** and countless of women all around the world who are descendants of Eve, each with their own stories to tell.

Eve's story lives on, and even though the struggles handed down have not been easy, we have many victorious stories of women who were able to overcome several trials and tragedies in life. It is important to note that Eve's story did not end as a victim of her circumstances. She persevered through adversity, pursuing the promise of God. There's a call to be better than our present conditions, to be better than what our past says about us, to be better than what life handed us—called to be stronger and more courageous than the women who came before us. Even though, some of us are still seeking redemption from the days where the fruit of the tree of knowledge haunts our actions, haunts our ability to love, haunts our ability to have fruitful relationships, disturbs our ability to give life, and haunts our ability to live purposefully. Eve never stopped seeking to overcome her deception through the power of redemption. She lived in the hope of being redeemed, as she remembered the promise of God: A child will be born that will crush the head of the Serpent and redeem all the inhabitants of the earth.

Being Eve Lesson 8

I lived a purpose driven life. Although I experienced tragedy and pain, it did not stop me from living the life I was called to sustain. The greatest deception in the world is the thought that if you made mistakes, who you are and what you were created to do is no longer valid. This couldn't be further from the truth. Adam and Eve's mistake disqualified them from living in the Garden, but it didn't disqualify their purpose. They had work to do, they wanted to get back to that Garden, and only fulfilling the promise of God would get them back there. **(Isaiah 9:6-7)**

CASEY ALEXIS

CHAPTER 9

THE REDEMPTION IN MOTION

I would be remiss to close out this book and end, Eve's story with her seeking redemption and not disclose the day she received it. The redemption plans spoken not too long after the fall, detailed a strategy where one day Eve's offspring would finally repay the serpent for its deception. Genesis, 3:15 states, ***"And I will put enmity between you and the woman, and between your offspring and hers; he will crush your head, and you will strike his heel."*** This plan was set into motion as soon as God spoke those words. Reminiscent of what took place when He spoke the earth into existence, God put a plan in motion, not only to redeem Adam and Eve but to redeem the entire world. This plan was essential to Eve as it indicated expressly that her offspring would crush her enemy's head. Also, as stated in the previous chapter, it kept her operating in her calling despite all the tragedies experienced. As we delve into this chapter, hold on tight, because we are going to skip across a couple of generations to the greatest story ever told.

As do most of us who experience hardship, we hope for a day where life can finally be kind to us and give us a happy ending. Eve looked forward to that day God promised, and it happened generations later in a town called Bethlehem, through a virgin named Mary **(Luke 1:26-38)**. The biblical foretelling of the birth of Jesus was purposeful in revealing God's intent to redeem humanity. The way Jesus Christ entered the earth was truly significant to the plan of redemption foretold by God in Genesis 3:15. Just like when God fashioned Eve from Adam's rib, Jesus had to come from life, hence why he had to be born from a woman. The moment of his conception did not take place through the act of intercourse. It happened through Mary's willingness to be a vessel to carry him gestationally. He was not made through the seed of an Adam (Joseph), so the tree of knowledge of good and evil was not genetically passed on to him. He came directly from God, and as the Son of God, he entered the world through a woman. Making him human, but also fully divine.

As previously discussed in the earlier chapters, Adam and Eve each had a specific purpose designed to establish life on earth. Keeping to that order, Jesus came from life (a woman) to redeem it, offering us all a new life through him. He was also born a male, allowing him the authority required to redeem the earth, because Adam was made from the ground. He covered both the purpose of the one who maintained (Adam) and the one who sustained (Eve). God was indeed purposeful and very specific on how this would all play out. Jesus came into the world in a very humble manner; he lived a straightforward life, up until he hit 30 years of age. The three years from the time his ministry began until the time he was put to death was action-packed. In that time, he spent his time restoring people amid their tragic stories and a ruthless government. He healed the sick, gave sight to the blind, expelled demons, raised the dead, and simultaneously stood up against pompous religious grandeur.

As we fast-forward through Jesus' life to focus on his death and resurrection, what was written in Genesis foreshadowed His coming. Jesus died, giving God his very best, offering himself, his purpose, and his life as a sacrifice. Unlike the blood of Abel, the blood of Jesus did not cry out to God in vain. Jesus cried out to God in agony as he took on the sins of the entire world, but the shedding of his blood-covered all, creating a clear path of redemption for all to seek refuge **(2 Corinthians 5:21)**. The death of Jesus took on everything the tree of knowledge of good and evil exposed us to-- Finally crushing the head of the serpent that deceived Eve long ago.

But the story didn't end there...God was not done. Access to the Tree of Life needed to be restored, and it could not come from the hands of a dead man. The resurrection of Jesus Christ was part of the redemption plan. As it was in the beginning with Adam and Eve, his resurrection opened the opportunity to choose life or death freely. ***"You are free to eat from any tree in the Garden, but you must not eat from the tree of the knowledge of good and evil, for when you eat from it, you will certainly die."*** To announce to the world that the choice was now available to all, God required life to declare that Jesus Christ was alive, and it began with a group of women who were followers of Jesus. They were impressed to go to the tomb and see where Jesus' body laid. When they got there, they learned from an Angel, that Jesus was no longer in the grave. As instructed, they went to go and tell the disciples that he had risen from the dead. On their way to tell the disciples, Jesus Christ himself greeted them and confirmed that He indeed was alive, and instructed them to tell the disciples where to meet him. **(Matthew 28:1-10)**

Jesus Christ appeared to the women who were at the tomb, is a glaring reminder that God's respect for His order is impeccable. He will not go out of His order even when He can. Although Christ's disciples spent countless amounts of intimate time with Jesus throughout his ministry, it was the women who were impressed upon to go to the tomb. Those women meeting Jesus Christ before they got to the disciples was no coincidence. I truly believe this was explicitly intended by God to show us as women, descendants of Eve, that redemption has come. Those who are the gateways of life on earth had to announce that Christ was not dead, he is alive! This specific act was the start of what soon became the great commission as instructed by Christ to His Apostles.

MY REFLECTION:

Jesus Christ came to redeem the world, so we could have access to the life that God intended in the beginning. We are still living in the fallen world of Adam, and our soul remains housed in a fallen body, but we don't have to live a fallen life. Through the acceptance of the redemption of Christ, we have access to the tree of life that not only helps us sustain and maintain in this fallen world, but we no longer fear death.

_____

_____

_____

_____

_____

_____

_____

_____

_____

_____

_____

_____

_____

_____

_____

_____

The great commission to go out into all the world and preach the gospel **(Matthew 28:19)**— literally changed the world! To this very day, the Gospel of Jesus Christ has transcended time, space, language, and culture. It all began with a young women's willingness to be a gateway to a life that allowed Christ to enter the world. The baby born in Bethlehem had a simple experience, and in three short years of his adulthood, he made such an impact that it changed the world. Then, from his death and resurrection, there was a group of redeemed women who operated in their authority as gateways of life to speak life into the hearts of the eleven men. Those men served in their power to preach the Gospel. Each one began to change the environments they entered, and it spread like wildfire--redemption had finally come.

Isn't it amazing that the deception began with a woman transferring it to the man, who, in turn, changed the world? But, the redemption of the world was announced by women, who then transferred it to a group of men who then began to change the world. God's perfect plan was complete, but His order remained the same.

Redemption through Jesus Christ removed the rulership and replaced it with a headship by our male counterparts, re-establishing God's perfect plan through Christ. *Galatians 3:23-29 (NIV), Before the coming of this faith, we were held in custody under the law, locked up until the faith that was to come would be revealed. So the law was our guardian until Christ came that we might be justified by faith. Now that this faith has come, we are no longer under a guardian. So in*

Christ Jesus, you are all children of God through faith, for all of you who were baptized into Christ have clothed yourselves with Christ. There is neither Jew nor Gentile, neither slave nor free, nor is there male and female, for you are all one in Christ Jesus. If you belong to Christ, then you are Abraham's seed, and heirs according to the promise.

We are gateways of life called to bring life in every area where the presence of women is made known—called to a life that leads with purpose, anointing, and authority in our families, in our homes, in the church, and the marketplace. We can have experiences that have value, not subjected to all forms of abuse, violence, and mistreatment—women who are fearfully made and designed with a purpose.

> ### *BEING EVE LESSON 9*
>
> ***God's timing is perfect.***
>
> I'm sure Eve desired redemption in her lifetime, but it didn't turn out that way. And this is where most of us, if not all of us struggle with God, it is in His timing. God's timing may not be perfect for us, but it is perfect for what He desires to accomplish in us. He doesn't do things with just one person in mind. God is a good father and a good father thinks about the generations to come. I am a firm believer that God doesn't move on a timeline that will only bless us, He is also very mindful of the generations that will come through us. So, trust Him and His timing.
>
> **(Proverbs 3:4-5)**

CASEY ALEXIS

CHAPTER 10

AS IT WAS IN THE BEGINNING

Imagine for a second what it must've been like to be born into a world made exclusively for a man...

I hope by the time you have gotten to this chapter, you have come to the realization that a world made exclusively for a man was not what God had in mind; in fact, He thought it was a terrible idea! And it certainly was not in the Spirit of God when He was putting together this beautiful masterpiece. Eve was never an afterthought when He created Adam. If you recall, Eve was formed from the rib of Adam, so she was with him the very day God breathed into Adam's nostrils. So, when the realization of man being alone wasn't a good thing, it was a simple act of creating Eve by taking a piece of what was already alive. Eve's physical existence was simply God separating the two, giving them distinct characteristics along with a definite purpose that worked so well together. It is a beautiful representation of what takes place when a man and woman willingly decide to journey into the calling of matrimony, the two becoming one—intricately designed within their separate callings to impact the world interchangeably and positively. The building, maintaining, and creating a sustainable life together, not only for themselves but for the generations that will come from their union.

When you look back at the creation story, you will realize how a simple shift of perception changed everything. The Serpent in the Garden of Eden changed Eve's perception, by merely asking a question that changed her outlook on her purpose and her attitude towards God. Sometimes, that's simply all it takes to change the way we feel and eventually change the way we act. The serpents of this world haven't changed much, and the tactics remain the same: Make a woman believe that she is less than, make her think that her purpose is less than, that her value is less than, and she will yearn to eat from strange fruit that is not to her benefit. The results will often have us giving of ourselves, our body, our gifts, and our power to those who are less deserving. Then there are those of us who continue to fight to level the playing field to gain equal footing with our male counterparts, attempting to define our purpose through the eyes of the creation rather than the Creator.

The fallen nature and the rulership of man over woman have made us accustomed to looking at our value through a male's perspective, continually searching for validation and acceptance at *their* table. When the only table we need to seek to be amongst is the table of redemption, if we continue to find our purpose from the hands of creation rather than the hands of the creator, we will continue to be devalued. When we look at the importance of women through God's point of view and what the redemption of Jesus Christ has finished, you will soon realize that the original intent of God's plan has been restored. Without women, men are not good alone. Without men, women are not good alone. We need each other; neither is higher than the other, neither needing to be ruled by another. But all under the subjection and the rulership of Christ, willingly able to submit to one another without question.

So, what about the headship, the Bible says the man is the head. Yes, the Bible is always right; the man is the head. And guess what you are to the head of your household (if it applies)? You are his helpmeet, his helper. He maintains, and you sustain. You are called to help him lead in life, the way the Lord intricately designed for you both. He no longer has to rule over you, because when you decided to accept Jesus Christ as your Lord and Savior, you renounced the ways of the world and received the gift of salvation. So, you hold your place, and he holds his and the two of you together are a dynamic duo!

Are you surprised? Well, you shouldn't be. I hope by now, you have come to the full understanding that this book was not given to me by me. It was a gift given to me that changed my life. I, in turn, return the favor by putting it to paper as God's original plan as a practical, applicable way for you to understand.

A woman births, a woman nurses and nurtures, a woman supports, provides wisdom, heals wounds, and loves so much so a person can feel empowered, encouraged, and secure. Ladies, we are a valuable source to the successful continuation of life on this planet. We add tremendous value to all facets of life because that is what we bring to the table—a vessel for life.

When you think about some of the greatest men in history that impacted the world with significant change, there was a woman that birthed him, raised him, and a woman eventually married him. She was right beside him, speaking life into his very existence, urging him to keep on going despite the challenges that he faced. There are also amazing women in history who met their challenges head-on when tragedy and disaster were attempting to overtake them. Women have led governments, held offices, ran companies, wrote books, created, and entertained, succeeded and thrived despite the odds. Yes, that is life-fighting to keep on moving. Let's not forget all the women who function at maximum capacity every day with the most challenging job and the most important calling in the world--the raising of children. We are an amazing part of God's plan. We are fearfully and wonderfully made to do extraordinary things. Our very presence is an announcement of God's masterpiece in creation. I genuinely hope that one day we can all embrace the fact that although we live in Adam's fallen world, it does not define who we are in Christ.

I end this book with two challenges.

CHALLENGE 1: I challenge you to put an end to viewing the value of your life through man's perspective, to stop looking at your life through the lens of creation, but rather the Creator.
You are more than any definition humanity attempts to use to define you:
You are not less!

You are not a mistake!

You are not a receptacle!

You are not a sex toy!

You are not a carpet to be walked on!

You are not a punching bag to be abused!

You are not a covering to any man!

You are not a door that can be opened and closed at whim!

You are not a product!

You are not a service!

You are not the rape in your story!

Your story of sexual abuse does not define you!

You are not the abortion you had!

You are not stupid!

You are not ugly!

You are not those hurtful words spoken over you!

You are a daughter of the Most-High God, fearfully fashioned in Him, redeemed through Jesus Christ to bring life and to sustain life in every facet of experience in this world!

CHALLENGE 2: I challenge you to begin to look at your life through God's point of view. A place of a higher purpose and authority.

You are a child of God!

You are loved!

You are fearfully and wonderfully made!

You are a giver of life!

You are a sustainer!

You are accepted!

You are free!

You are chosen!

You are no longer a slave to sin!

You have a purpose!

You are forgiven!

You are more precious than jewels!

You are a crown to the one you love!

You are beautiful!

You are brilliant!

You are a light to the world!

As you meditate and meet these challenges daily, I want to remind you of a story. There is a woman in scripture named Mary Magdalene, not to be confused with Mary, the mother of Jesus. Mary Magdalene had a past; she was a prostitute, and one day her past came to confront her in the form of men crowding around to stone her to death. Thankfully, it just so happens Jesus was in the midst, and he did something intriguing... he began to write on the ground, and that stopped everyone in their tracks. He challenged the men with their stones: those who had no sin in their lives to be the first to knock good ole Mary Magdalene to the ground. Well, if you can imagine it, no one came forward. Jesus then looked at Mary and said in **John 8:11, "...Go now and leave your life of sin."**

So, Mary Magdalene got up that day, followed Christ, and NEVER looked back.

So, I end this chapter, to proclaim the new life that God has given us an all-access path through Christ, no longer having to live as an entity satisfying the desires of creation but instead to live our lives through God's point of view. A higher calling, a greater perspective.

So, go now and live!

BEING EVE LESSON 10

I am who God says I am.

The greatest lesson to learn from Eve in all of this is to never allow the serpents of this world to question who God says you are. The moment you begin to question your value and your worth is the moment you begin to lose the footing you have in Christ. One of the greatest lines in scripture is a verse where Jesus responds to the "serpents," of his time when he was questioned about who He was. He replies and says, **"Even if I testify on my own behalf, my testimony is valid, for I know where I came from and where I am going..."** Knowing who you are and what you have been called to do creates a boundary that most won't dare to cross. And for those who will attempt to challenge you, they will be met with a fierce battle they will lose, because you do not stand alone. **(John 8:14-16)**

MY REFLECTION:

Who does GOD say you are?

NOTES

NOTES

NOTES

NOTES

INDEX

The Function of the Bone

https://www.cliffsnotes.com/study-guides/anatomy-and-physiology/bones-and-skeletal-tissues/functions-of-bones

Scriptural References:

Holy Bible

New International Version. Zondervan, 1984

www.ingramcontent.com/pod-product-compliance
Lightning Source LLC
Chambersburg PA
CBHW051131160426
43195CB00014B/2434